W9-ATK-269

Eager Street Academy #884
401 East Eager Street
Baltimore, MD 21202

Property of: / Title I
Baltimore City / Title Program
Baltimore and Delinquent Year 2022-2023
Neglected School Year 2022-2023 Academy/#884
Eager Street Academy

Poverty

Critical World Issues

CRITICAL WORLD ISSUES

Poverty

Karen Steinman

MASON CREST
PHILADELPHIA

Mason Crest
450 Parkway Drive, Suite D
Broomall, PA 19008
www.masoncrest.com

©2017 by Mason Crest, an imprint of National Highlights, Inc.

Printed and bound in the United States of America.

CPSIA Compliance Information: Batch #CWI2016.
For further information, contact Mason Crest at 1-866-MCP-Book.

3 5 7 9 8 6 4 2

Library of Congress Cataloging-in-Publication Data

on file at the Library of Congress
ISBN: 978-1-4222-3658-1 (hc)
ISBN: 978-1-4222-8138-3 (ebook)

Critical World Issues series ISBN: 978-1-4222-3645-1

Table of Contents

KEY ICONS TO LOOK FOR:

Words to Understand: These words with their easy-to-understand definitions will increase the reader's understanding of the text, while building vocabulary skills.

Sidebars: This boxed material within the main text allows readers to build knowledge, gain insights, explore possibilities, and broaden their perspectives by weaving together additional information to provide realistic and holistic perspectives.

Research Projects: Readers are pointed toward areas of further inquiry connected to each chapter. Suggestions are provided for projects that encourage deeper research and analysis.

Text-Dependent Questions: These questions send the reader back to the text for more careful attention to the evidence presented there.

Series Glossary of Key Terms: This back-of-the book glossary contains terminology used throughout this series. Words found here increase the reader's ability to read and comprehend higher-level books and articles in this field.

What Is Poverty?

oxana lives with her family in south-central Los Angeles. In many ways, 15-year-old Roxana is lucky. She has a loving family and two parents living at home. She is one of the best students in her class and wants to go to college to study law. So, what's the problem?

The problem is that Roxana comes from a poor family in one of the most deprived areas in a rich city, and this will affect her opportunities in life.

Let us take school as an example. Roxana is a keen student and her parents want her to do well. But the local schools are old and decaying. Roxana's high school was built for 1,000 students, but today it has three times that number. She says, "There are not enough books and computers, and classes are too crowded. It's impossible to talk to a teacher on your own, there are so many other students."

An Indian woman with her children in their rural village. Roughly 400 million people in South Asia are considered to be living in "absolute poverty," or surviving on less than US $1.25 per day.

Who can study in such an environment? Not surprisingly, many students drop out. Some join gangs or roam the streets, some go to jail, some even get killed. Only about one-third actually stay in school to receive their high school diploma. Yet, without this precious piece of paper, it is impossible to get a good job or go on to college.

Even those who stay, like Roxana, have huge difficulties. To go to college, students must study chemistry. But while there are plenty of classes in subjects like cooking, floor-covering, and make-up, there are only a few classes for chemistry. It is difficult to get career advice and to prepare for exams. No wonder most students drop out.

Meanwhile, in wealthy west Los Angeles, students attend schools with small classes, good equipment and interesting subjects. Nearly every student will go on to college, which their

 Words to Understand in This Chapter

absolute poverty—when people lack the basic things needed to survive.

bigha—a measure of land, used in India and Bangladesh.

charity—a group or organization that aims to help people or provide a service without making a profit.

discrimination—treating people differently and unfairly because of their gender, race or ethnic background, or way of life.

op shop—Australian term for charity or second-hand shop.

relative poverty—when people lack the basic things needed to live a good life in their society.

sanitation—hygienic ways of disposing of rubbish and human waste.

Roxanna lives in a poor neighborhood in south-central Los Angeles.

parents will pay for, and later they will get good jobs. Even if Roxana does get to college, she will have to work to pay her fees and living expenses.

Roxana knows that her parents want her to have the opportunities they never had. She says: "My father grew up in a village in Guatemala where no children went to school, and many people never learned to read and write. Twenty years ago, he made a long, dangerous journey north. It took three attempts before he could cross the border into the United States, and years of casual work before he found his job as a janitor. It doesn't pay much and the hours are long, but at least he has some security."

Although life in south-central Los Angeles is tough, Roxana's parents know that life is much harder in Guatemala. In their village there had been no running water, no electricity, and no medical clinics.

Around 60 percent of the people who live in south-central Los Angeles are Hispanic—Spanish-speakers from Mexico and Central America. Many others are African Americans, or members of other ethnic minority groups. They all face *discrimination* in education and employment. Even though they live in one of the world's wealthiest cities, poverty affects their lives.

What Is Poverty?

We all think we understand the meaning of the words "rich" and "poor." To be "rich" means that you have plenty of good things—perhaps even more than you need—and to be "poor" means you do not have enough, or perhaps any, of the same things. But how do we decide whether someone is rich or poor?

Look at the lists on the following pages. Starting with the first list, "Your Things," decide what things are necessary for you to live a good life, what things would make you feel "rich" and what things would make you feel "poor." Are there other things you would add to the list of what things are necessary, and why would you include them?

Now do the same exercise, using the lists for "Your Family" (page 11) and "Your Community" (page 12). How do the three lists compare with each other? Do you think that there are some things that every single person should have, regardless of who they are or whether they are rich or poor? Now, draw up your own list of the things you think are necessary, starting with the most important and ending with the least important.

Your Things

- A computer or tablet
- Books, pens and pencils
- A mobile phone
- A video game console
- A pair of sneakers
- A pair of plastic sandals
- New clothes every month
- New clothes every year
- Your own bed
- Your own bedroom
- Pocket money for doing work around the home
- Pocket money without doing any work

Your Family

- A dishwasher
- A car
- Two cars
- A donkey and a cart
- A bank account
- One or more credit cards
- Three regular meals a day
- One regular meal a day
- A television set
- A television set in each room
- Holidays away from home every year
- Holidays staying at home every year

Your community

- Running water in every home
- Running water from taps in the street
- Electric lighting in every home
- Electric lighting in every street
- Regular public transport
- Old and unreliable public transport
- Regular rubbish collection
- Free healthcare for everyone
- Healthcare you pay for each time you go to the doctor's office
- A good school, free and open to everyone
- A good school, where everyone has to pay fees
- A not-so-good school, for people who cannot afford to pay

Is Poverty Different in Different Countries?

Jack from Australia and Abu Hameed from Bangladesh, in Asia, are both 11 years old. What do you think their stories tell you about being rich and poor?

Jack feels different from the other children in his class. Those children have lots of nice things—clothes, games, computers. Jack's mother buys his clothes from the *op shop* (a *charity* shop), and he uses a computer at the local library. His mother says not to worry—he is bright and is doing well at school. Still, Jack never invites other children home, and he wishes he had a room of his own. He believes he would not feel so bad if everyone was in the same situation.

Abu Hameed belongs to one of the richest families in his village. His father owns ten *bighas* of land, and has two cows and a plow. His family of six live in a three-room house, made of concrete with a tin roof. They have a radio and electric light, although the electricity supply often fails. His mother collects water from the village well, just like everyone else does. Abu Hameed

The children in almost any public school classroom will come from a wide range of backgrounds, meaning that some will come from much poorer families than others.

A farmer plows a field in Bangladesh. In this Asian country, a family that owns livestock and good land might be considered wealthy.

attends primary school and may go on to secondary school.

Who Is Poorer?

Jack has more possessions than Abu Hameed and his home has electricity and running water. He knows he will go to secondary school. One day he expects to have his own computer, maybe a car as well. But compared to the other pupils in his school, Jack looks and feels poor, and he is ashamed of his poverty.

Poverty in Three Countries

Poverty is a major problem in many parts of the world, especially in less-developed countries like those below.

GUATEMALA

Guatemala is a beautiful country, but very poor. Many farms are so tiny that each year farmers have to travel to the coffee plantations to work. They are paid low wages and work in terrible conditions.

BANGLADESH

Most land in Bangladesh is very fertile. But there are many people and there is not enough land to support everyone. So, each year people migrate to the big cities where they find work in the clothing factories.

ZAMBIA

Zambia is one of Africa's poorest countries. Many people do not live in villages but in sprawling shantytowns around the big cities. These do not have basic services like running water or rubbish collection.

A Haitian woman prepares "clay cakes," sun-baked disks made from mud, butter, and salt, which are sold in markets around Port-au-Prince for about 10 cents. Clay cakes have become a symbol of Haiti's struggles with extreme poverty and hunger.

Abu Hameed looks and feels confident. Although he does not have as much as Jack, and has never seen a computer, his family is prosperous and respected by other villagers. One day he will take over his father's role as head of the family.

These stories show how poverty and wealth can mean different things in different countries. Poverty is about much more than what you can afford to do or buy. It is also about

Shantytowns where poor people live in squalid, cramped conditions often rise up aroun[d] modern cities in many countries of Asia and Africa. These houses are in a poor neigh[bor]hood of Jakarta, Indonesia.

whether you feel part of society, and whether you can join in with other people.

How Do We Measure Poverty?

As we have seen, poverty means different things in different countries. What is regarded as poverty in a wealthy country such as Australia is different from poverty in a poor country such as Bangladesh. This is called *relative poverty*.

The United Nations (UN) tries to measure the numbers of people living in the worst poverty—what it calls *absolute poverty*. In simple language, absolute poverty occurs when people lack the basic things needed to live. These include enough food, safe drinking water, *sanitation*, healthcare, shelter, education, and access to media information via radio, television, or online. The UN estimates that of the world's 7.3 billion people, around 1.5 billion—more than 20 percent—live in absolute poverty. In money terms, these people survive on less than US$1.25 a day. That amount has to cover everything—food and drink, housing, clothes, travel, medicine, repaying debts and emergencies.

Who lives in absolute poverty?

Most of these 1.5 billion people live in Africa and Asia, especially India, Pakistan and Bangladesh. Around 70 percent are women and girls. Many cannot read or write. Most do not have regular income or employment, and when they do their earnings are tiny. Most own very little—usually just their clothes, some personal possessions and a few pots, pans and tools. If they fall ill or are injured, they must rely on their family to help. Many are in debt.

Let us look at just one of these 1.5 billion people—nine-year-old Namwinga from Zambia, in Africa. She lives with her aunt and cousins in a tiny, one-room home in a neighborhood called Chipata on the outskirts of the capital, Lusaka. Her mother died two years ago. Now her auntie supports all the children by selling vegetables in the market. Her aunt treats Namwinga well but there is never enough income or enough food. There is certainly not enough to pay school fees for all the children. So, each day Namwinga stays home, fetches water, and minds the smaller children. She will need to find paid work when she is older, but without schooling she has no hope of getting a well-paid job.

Some families in Chipata are slightly better off, and manage to save, move to a bigger house and buy furniture and a radio. Although these families are poor, they do not live in absolute poverty like Namwinga. But often the dividing line is very thin—all it takes is an illness or accident to plunge a whole family back into absolute poverty.

Text-Dependent Questions

1. What percentage of the people who live in south-central Los Angeles are Hispanic?
2. What are the conditions in which absolute poverty occurs?
3. What percentage of the world's population lives in absolute poverty, according to the United Nations?

 Research Project

Using your school library or the Internet, do some research to answer the question, "Is it better to live in a wealthy society, or a less-wealthy society?" Keep in mind that there are benefits to both. There may be larger gaps between rich and poor people in a wealthy society, but people in a wealthy society tend to have a higher standard of living. In a less-wealthy society, there are smaller gaps between rich and poor people, and wealth tends to be shared more equally. Write a two-page paper with your answer, using examples from your research to support your conclusion, and present it to your class.

Why are People Poor?

Why are some people poorer than others? Is it because they are too lazy to work? Is it because they cannot earn enough? Maybe they have too many children or live in a bad area. Or is it just a matter of luck? What other explanations can you think of?

In the previous chapter we saw that there are different ways of measuring poverty. Poverty in a rich country is clearly different from poverty in a poor country. But despite the differences, there are still things in common.

Almost everywhere, poor people come from families with a low or irregular income. In other words, if a child starts life in a poor family, he or she is more likely to grow up in poverty. Poor children eat less healthy food, live in crowded, low-quality housing and are at greater risk from illness. Their families

There are many reasons why some people, like this former American soldier, end up living in poverty and having to beg for a living.

have little money for good food, nice clothes, furniture, books, toys, holidays and the other things that help to ensure children have a good childhood.

Poor families usually live in areas with fewer *facilities* for young people, such as parks, sports grounds, swimming pools and clubs. There are fewer jobs and businesses, fewer shops and unreliable public transport. People feel trapped and stressed. No wonder that some people turn to crime, begging and violence.

How Are Poverty and Education Linked?

A good education, leading to a high-paying job, is one way out of poverty. You might think that everyone has an equal chance at school. But a child from a poor family rarely has the same opportunities as a child from a better off family. Even when

 Words to Understand in This Chapter

benefits—government social security payments.

contraception—methods used to prevent a woman becoming pregnant.

facilities—resources, buildings or equipment that bring services to people.

pension—a payment to an ill or retired person.

social security—payments by the government to people who are ill, disabled, unemployed or caring for family members.

vaccination—a treatment which prevents diseases such as measles, mumps and chickenpox.

A good education is an important step on the road out of poverty. These students are listening to their teacher in their school in the village of Bouaflé, Côte d'Ivoire.

schooling is free, parents have to buy clothes, books, sports gear and other extras.

In the poorest countries, many children do not attend school at all, or drop out early. In richer societies, all children attend primary and secondary school and many go on to college or university. But schools in poorer areas have bigger classes, less choice of subjects and fewer books and computers. So, learning becomes more difficult. And if children fall behind at

In the United States and many other developed countries, government agencies operate employment bureaus that help people to find jobs. They also pay unemployment compensation to people who have lost a job through no fault of their own; this temporary income is meant to help them make ends meet until they can find a new job. However, in poorer countries people who do not work do not receive this kind of support.

school, there is much less chance that they will catch up later.

Of course, not everyone born into poverty stays poor. Many people strive to get a good education, new skills, a better job or a move to another area. Many more benefit from changes in society—such as a booming economy creating more jobs, or government programs improving education. The world is full of people who were born into poverty, but have better, more secure lives than their parents.

Are Poor People Lazy?

How often have you heard someone say, "Of course some people are poor. There are jobs around but they don't want to work." How true is this statement?

Most developed countries, including the United States and Canada, have "safety nets" to protect people who cannot work. In wealthier countries, sick and unemployed people may receive *social security* payments from the government, and retired people receive *pensions*.

Without proper education and training, it is hard for even the most hardworking person to find a job that pays enough to support a family.

But in many developing countries, poor people have to work for a living because they have no other way of surviving. They own little or nothing of value, they have no savings and they receive no social *benefits* from the government. It is difficult to borrow money, because few people will lend it to them.

Women work on a farm in the country of East Timor in southeast Asia. A United Nations report once stated, "Women are half the world's population, yet they do two-thirds of the world's work, receive one-tenth of the world's income, and own less than one-hundredth of the world's property."

If they do receive a loan it comes with a high rate of interest, and they must find a way of repaying it. The only safety net they have is support from family members or close friends, but usually they are just as badly off.

Are Women Poorer than Men?

All over the world, the poorest women do the hardest work, for the longest hours and for the lowest wages. Often they do "double days"—working inside and outside the home. For example, let us look at Devi, who lives in a village in India. Her day starts at 4 AM, as she walks in darkness to the village well, where she must collect the water she needs for cooking and washing. Devi returns home carrying this heavy load, careful not to spill the precious water. Every day, Devi cuts the vegetables and grinds the spices for family meals. There is no gas or electricity, just a mud stove, so meals take hours to cook. She collects firewood, milks the cow and sweeps the mud floors, all the time keeping an eye on the children.

Devi also works in the fields, planting, watering and weeding the rice seedlings. At harvest time, she not only works long hours under the hot sun, but continues doing her "woman's work," carrying water and cooking. The women in the village rise earlier and go to sleep later than everyone else.

Devi works seven days a week. Her only breaks come when there is a religious festival, or a traveling fair comes to the village. Even then, she must get water and cook for the family. Devi is clearly not lazy, and yet the only things she owns are her clothes and some jewelry. She does not even think about the future, or whether things will get better for her.

More children means more helping hands for this poor family in South Sudan.

Do Poor People Have Too Many Children?

There are many reasons why people want children. Parents may simply enjoy family life, or they may want children to carry on the family name. It is natural to want children, but do poor people have too many? Is this the reason why they live in poverty?

In certain societies, parents hope to have many children. In rural areas of these societies, children are able to add to the family income through their work. They help out at home, work in the fields, herd animals, and look after younger siblings. But as people move into towns and cities, families tend to become smaller. City children are more likely to attend school, and this can be expensive for parents. Modern methods of *contraception* enable parents to have more control over the size of their family, though this decision is also affected by religion and custom. But city-dwellers, rich and poor, generally have fewer children than families in the countryside.

Not so long ago, many children died when they were babies or toddlers. They died of diseases due to living in unhealthy conditions, or from complications related to poverty, such as hunger. Today we know how to deal with these things, through better hygiene, modern medicines, *vaccinations* against diseases, and nutritious food. As more children survive, parents feel less need to have as many children.

Why Do Children Die of Poverty?

Today, fewer children die than in the past. However, there is still a big difference between children's health in rich and poor countries. In rich countries, almost all children can expect to have a healthy childhood and to reach adulthood. In the poorest countries, around one in four children die before they are five years old. Even when food and medicines are available, their parents cannot afford to buy them. These children die of poverty.

Birth rates are now falling as parents all over the world choose to have fewer children. This is true in rich and poor countries alike, although birth rates are still higher in poor

A homeless man pushes a cart with all of his possessions.

countries and poor people still have more children than richer ones.

However, having more children does not make people poor. They have more children because they are poor. If they become more prosperous, if fewer children die early and if more children have the opportunity to stay in school for a longer time, then parents nearly always choose to have fewer, but healthier, children.

 ## Text-Dependent Questions

1. What is one way for people to escape from poverty?
2. Why is it difficult for poor people to borrow money?

 ## Research Project

Using your school library or the Internet, do some research to answer the question, "Should people be forced to have fewer children?" Some will argue that government should stop people from having large families, because more people means more poverty and the world is already overpopulated. Others will contend that governments should not interfere with family decisions, even if the people live in poverty. Write a two-page paper with your answer, using examples from your research to support your conclusion, and present it to your class.

3

Is Poverty a Worldwide Problem?

T he United Nations and other organizations have studied whether the world is becoming richer or poorer. Although the answers are very complex, they can be summarized fairly simply: the world is getting both richer and poorer at the same time.

Today, more people than ever before have enough to eat and drink, live in adequate housing, get a good education and live healthy lives. But there are also many more people than ever before without these things. While some countries have the means to provide every person with the good things of life, many other countries struggle to provide for even the basic needs of their citizens, such as food and clean water.

As noted previously, around 1.5 billion of the world's 7.3 billion people live in absolute poverty. Most of these people live

←——————————————————————

Hungry people look for food or useful items in a garbage dump near Maputo, Mozambique. Some of the world's poorest countries are in Africa, and the poorest people have the fewest resources.

in Africa and Asia; some live in Latin America and Eastern Europe; and a few even live in the wealthiest countries, including the United States and Canada.

Of the 193 countries that belong to the United Nations, 48 are classified as "least developed countries," or LDCs. These are the world's poorest countries, which need special efforts to help them out of poverty. In 2016, the list of LDCs included Afghanistan, Haiti, Sierra Leone, and Yemen. When it comes to industrialization, education, and other modern economic measures, the gap between the wealthiest and poorest countries is so vast that it is hard to see how the LDCs could ever catch up.

How Is the World's Wealth Shared Out?

The richest 20 percent of the world's people possess 80 percent of the wealth, measured in money and goods. This means that

 Words to Understand in This Chapter

chronic—deep-rooted, persistent.

interest rates—an extra amount that must be paid when repaying a loan or debt.

malnutrition—the lack of foods necessary for good health.

market economy—the system of buying, selling, and exchanging goods for money.

subsidies—money paid by the government to keep the price of certain goods or products lower.

tariff—extra taxes or payments that are required, often on goods that have been manufactured or produced in another country.

In the developed world, even families that do not consider themselves "wealthy" have access to tablet computers and other technology, not to mention fresh and healthy food. These countries use a disproportionate share of the world's resources.

the other 80 percent of people must share the remaining 20 percent of the wealth. Even more shocking is the fact that the poorest 20 percent of the world's people own less than 1 percent of the world's wealth.

There is another factor to consider. Many of the Earth's resources are being used so rapidly that there may be nothing left for future generations. Population growth, along with the developed world's demands for more and more goods, take an increasing toll on forests, farmlands, seas, and rivers, as well as oil, gas, and mineral deposits. And the worst shortages are in

In recent years, severe droughts in Africa have put millions of poor farmers, such as this man from Niger, at risk of starvation.

the poorest countries.

What Is Hunger?

According to the United Nations World Food Programme, every day almost 800 million people—approximately 1 of every nine people in the world—go hungry. But what exactly do we mean by hunger?

Sometimes hunger is obvious: when rain doesn't fall, crops fail and people begin to starve. We see television images of people living in countries hit with droughts who have wasted, stunted bodies and large, staring eyes. This is the extreme face of hunger, but it is only part of the story.

The fact is that most of the 800 million hungry people do not appear on our television screens. These people suffer from *chronic malnutrition*, a hidden hunger. They do not eat enough food, and the food that they do get is not nourishing. Without good food, children cannot survive and grow into healthy adults. Without enough food, adults cannot work and support their families. They do not starve, but they do not thrive either.

Is There Enough Food to Feed Everyone?

Worldwide, there is no shortage of food. In fact, there is more than enough food to feed all 7 billion people who currently live

 Calculating the Cost

In Ethiopia, a country in eastern Africa, the average family has seven children. In the United States, the average family has only two children. Does this mean that an Ethiopian family places a much greater burden on the Earth's precious resources? The answer is no. During his or her lifetime, a child in the United States consumes 50 times more resources (food, clothes, computers, furniture, fuel for transport) than a child in Ethiopia. So, although an Ethiopian family is bigger, they use only a fraction of the resources of an American family.

Soybeans are harvested on a large plantation in Brazil. The implementation of advanced technology on farms in the developed world, along with better understanding of how to maximize crop yields, has led to an increase in the amount of food that is produced each year. Despite this bounty, many people around the world continue to go hungry.

on Earth. However, whether we have food in our stomachs depends on how much food costs and how much we earn. All around the world, the poorest groups spend the highest percentage of their income on food, while the richest spend a much smaller proportion.

Over the last decade, the money paid to farmers for their products has fallen, yet the price of food in the supermarkets and grocery stores has risen. Farmers must become more efficient and produce more food just to earn the same amount of money. The poorest farmers have little left over once they've sold their crops and animals, as most of their earnings go to pay fees and taxes and to repay loans.

Despite farmers receiving less money, prices in the supermarkets rise as governments cut *subsidies* on basic foods. Workers and small traders, whose wages have not risen, have to pay higher prices for staple foods such as rice, maize, and beans. Increasingly, the poorest people go hungry. The result is greater hunger and greater poverty.

Does World Trade Cause Poverty?

In the past most people were self-sufficient—growing and catching their own food, making their own clothes, and building their own homes. They did well in some years, but suffered in times of drought or flood. But today most people are linked to the wider world of buying, selling, and earning money, which is known as the *market economy*.

The market economy offers billions of people access to all sorts of different goods, many of which can make their lives better. Even in the poorest communities there are usually factory-made goods—such as clothes, batteries, tools, and plastic buckets—some of which have been imported from countries on the other side of the world.

Most people earn money either by selling goods, or by working for themselves or others. But with many people all trying to do the same thing, competition is fierce. This forces prices down, so workers earn even less. The low wages, of course, make it harder for the workers to buy the goods they need to survive.

Is the Market Economy Fair?

Often, worldwide competition is neither equal nor fair. The wealthiest countries have advantages—better technology, bigger markets, and lower transport costs—which make it difficult for poor countries to compete. The most powerful countries also protect their own industries by supporting them with subsidies, and imposing *tariffs* to keep out goods from poorer countries.

Let us look at how world trade affects just one little girl in Guatemala. Seven-year-old Rosa lives with her family in a tiny mountain village. Every year, they migrate to the coastal plains to work on big coffee plantations. Wages are low and conditions are terrible, but it is the only way that the family can survive. Even Rosa must pick coffee beans.

Even when the world price of coffee is high, the wages for workers are low. But since 2011, the world price of coffee has fallen by almost 60 percent. The growers now get less, and so do the coffee pickers. So, Rosa and her family face worse poverty. They will cut back on food, Rosa will not start school, and if someone falls sick there will be no medicine.

Surprisingly, the cost of coffee in the shops and cafés has fallen while the demand for coffee has increased. Growers who provide "green" (unroasted) coffee beans only receive 7 to 10 percent of the final cost of the coffee, while most of the profit goes to factories and retailers in wealthy countries. So, even while trade and profits boom, Rosa's family becomes poorer.

A female laborer tends young coffee bushes on a plantation in Antigua, Guatemala.

Is Government Debt a Problem?

The poorest countries face other problems. Some are involved in wars that cost money and lives. Some have corrupt or undemocratic governments, whose rule benefits only a tiny minority. Even peaceful countries with democratic governments often lack the resources to make a difference to people's lives.

But one of the biggest problems for poor countries is debt—the money they owe to governments or banks in developed countries. Many countries borrowed money 20 or 30 years ago,

A Ugandan child carries water bottles to collect fresh water for his family. Although conditions have improved in Uganda over the past two decades, it remains one of the poorest countries in Africa.

when *interest rates* were low. As interest rates rose, their repayments grew larger. As governments try to repay their debts, they must often reduce their spending on areas such as health, education, and sanitation. This means that the poorest people miss out on the very things that could improve their lives.

How Does Government Debt Affect People?

One of the 48 "least developed countries" is Uganda, in eastern Africa. Uganda is a fertile land with hardworking people, but it has suffered from decades of war and corruption. Farmers grow coffee and tea for export, and when international prices for these commodities are high—as they were in 2011 and 2012—revenue from the sale of these products helps the government to pay off some of the country's debts. However, coffee prices have mostly been low over the past two decades.

In the early 2000s, the world's seven wealthiest countries made an agreement with Uganda. They agreed to cancel around 40 percent of Uganda's debts, if the government would spend the savings on health and education. The Ugandan government built 10,000 new classrooms, and abolished school fees so even the poorest children could attend. In 2005, Uganda's public debt dropped to less than 20 percent of the value of the country's gross domestic product (the total value of goods and services produced within Uganda in a year). It seemed that Uganda might finally take steps out of poverty.

However, the Ugandan government has continued to borrow money to finance its economy. By 2015, the country's debt

An Ethiopian woman holds teff, a grain that is the primary subsistence crop in Ethiopia.

had once again risen, to more than $7 billion—more than 35 percent of its GDP. Uganda's annual interest payments on its debt increased from $179 million to more than $300 million, reducing the amount of government revenue that can be used to provide education or health care, or maintain roads and infrastructure. As a result, it remains very hard for poor Ugandans to escape debt and build a good life.

 Text-Dependent Questions

1. How many countries does the United Nations classify as "least developed countries," or LDCs?

2. How do wealthy countries protect their own industries?

 Research Project

Using your school library or the Internet, do some research to answer the question, "Should poor countries pay back debts to rich countries?" Keep in mind there may be legitimate arguments on both sides. Some experts say that when a country borrows money it should be required to pay it back, whatever the cost, and that canceling debts will permit governments to behave irresponsibly and run up even larger debts. Other experts believe that canceling a poor country's debt gives it a chance for a new start, and benefits the poor residents who would suffer most if services are cut. Write a two-page paper with your answer, using examples from your research to support your conclusion, and present it to your class.

How Does Poverty Affect Daily Life?

Although poverty affects all age groups, babies and children are especially affected. Because they are small, they are more vulnerable to cold, heat, dirt, disease, hunger and violence. And unlike adults, who can generally provide for themselves, young children are dependent for their survival on others.

Poverty affects a person's health and welfare even before they are born. If a pregnant woman has enough food, a safe environment and regular medical care, she has a good chance of having a healthy baby. However, if she lacks nourishing food, works long hours at heavy tasks and has no medical care, then she is likely to have a small, less healthy baby.

How Does Poverty Affect Children?

In poor countries, babies and toddlers die from common infections and illnesses, such as diarrhea, chest infections, measles

Poor people in Delhi, India, line up for a free meal.

and mumps. In tropical countries, malaria is one of the biggest killers of young children. Sometimes there are simple, low-cost ways to deal with these illnesses, such as sugar and salt solutions for diarrhea, but medicines are often not available. The good news is that most children are now vaccinated against killer diseases.

Poor children are often malnourished. Not only do they not have enough food, they do not have the right sort of food with the vitamins and minerals needed for healthy growth. Poorly nourished children are small for their age and may have learning difficulties. Millions of children in Asia and Africa suffer from *vitamin A* deficiency, which leads to bad eyesight and blindness.

As poor children survive and grow, they face different dangers. Accidents are common, especially from hot cooking pots on open fires, and increasingly from heavy traffic. Children who drop out of school often take hard, dangerous jobs unsuitable for their growing bodies. Without education, young people have less opportunity to learn how to protect their health. This

 Words to Understand in This Chapter

HIV/AIDS—HIV (Human Immuno-deficiency Virus) infection leads to AIDS (Acquired Immune Deficiency Syndrome), an illness in which the body's protective systems break down.

inflation—when money rapidly loses its value.

vitamin A deficiency—a lack of vitamin A in a person's diet.

Raw sewage flows through a ditch next to this street that runs through a slum in Agra, India. The stagnant, polluted waters are a breeding ground for diseases.

makes them more vulnerable to diseases and less aware of the potential dangers of "high-risk" behavior—be it taking drugs or exposing themselves to the risk of *HIV/AIDS*.

According to the World Health Organization (WHO), more than 6.3 million children under the age of five died in 2013. More than half of these early child deaths were due to conditions that could be prevented or treated with access to simple, affordable interventions. The leading causes of death included preterm birth complications, pneumonia, birth asphyxia, diar-

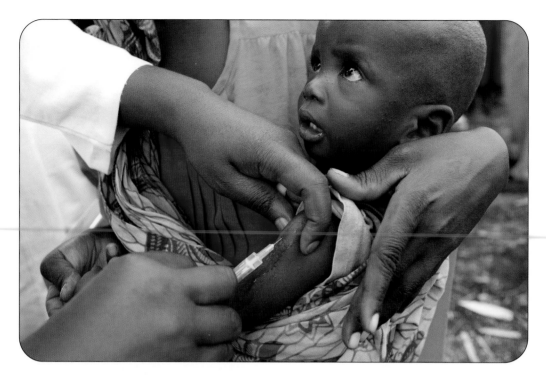

A doctor working with the World Health Organization vaccinates a child against measles in the Democratic Republic of the Congo.

rhea, and malaria. About 45 percent of all child deaths were linked to malnutrition. The WHO found that children in sub-Saharan Africa were more than 15 times more likely to die before the age of five than children in developed countries.

How Do People Get Enough to Live On?

It is hard to be poor. As we have seen, poverty takes different forms and it is often difficult to compare one country with another. But, wherever you live, poverty creates real practical problems in everyday life. The biggest single problem is always the same—being able to afford the basic things that your society considers essential for living. To do this, most people must work.

Most people look for a steady job with good, regular wages. But such jobs are not always available. They are especially hard to find for someone without a good education or special skills. Usually there are many people all trying to get the same job, and competition is fierce. And even if someone secures a steady job it does not necessarily mean they will be paid good wages.

Some people work with their families, farming, fishing or

Work comes in many forms. These Senegalese fishermen are unloading their day's catch at the dock in Darou Khoudoss.

Women work in a rice field in Nepal.

herding animals. Others have to make do with what work they can find—odd jobs here and there. In cities, poor people work in factories, in shops and on the streets, selling everything from food and drink, to good luck charms and lottery tickets. Others offer services—minding cars, carrying shopping and entertaining crowds. Some people make a living by singing songs, playing music or performing tricks. Others beg for money.

Work often involves traveling, but many people have to stay at home. This is true of women looking after small children or elderly relatives. Some are able to use their home as a work-place.

In some countries, poor children work as servants in the households of better off families and receive no wages at all—just food and a roof over their heads. Most work very long hours, and some are beaten and badly treated.

Sometimes people get payments from governments, such as social security benefits or pensions, especially in richer countries. These can be vital in helping people to survive, but they are often quite modest. In some countries, *inflation* has been so high that these government payments are not enough to provide the basic necessities.

How Does Poverty Affect Housing?

Poverty affects how and where people live, and their quality of life. Let us look at the stories of two girls—Luisa from Mozambique and Chloe from England. What do you think they have in common, and what are the differences?

Luisa is 10 years old and lives with her family in Polana Caniço A, a shantytown near Maputo, the capital city of Mozambique. The family shares a tiny two-room home, very similar to the thousands of others crowded into this small area. Nevertheless, Luisa's family are very proud of their home because they found the land and built the house themselves.

Luisa was born in Maputo. Her parents had fled to the capital from their village, to escape war and hunger. When they arrived, Polana Caniço A was a small collection of makeshift huts. Now, thousands of people live there and it has a school, health center, shops, restaurants, and churches. But most

homes do not have running water or electric light.

Chloe lives in a public housing complex, called a "council estate," in Newcastle upon Tyne, a big city in northern England. The house is much larger than Luisa's home; there's plenty of room for Chloe, her mother, and her two brothers, and the school is close by. But look a bit closer and things do not seem so good. Inside, the house is quite bare and there is not much furniture. Like almost every family that lives in the housing complex, Chloe's mother rents the house from the local government. The houses are modern but they already

(Opposite) Crowded shantytowns, or slums, can be found on the outskirts of most major cities in Africa, Asia, and South America. (Above) A British "council estate," or public housing development that is managed by the local government. Although such homes are often modest by western standards, they are far superior to the shacks in which poor people live in the developing world.

Schoolchildren in their classroom in the Kavango province, which has the highest poverty level in Namibia.

seem run down. Some are boarded up and empty, and a few have been burnt out or badly damaged.

Most families on Chloe's estate rely on government benefits. Many children grow up in jobless households and believe they will never have a job. Some turn to petty crime, vandalism, and drug-taking. That is one reason why Chloe's mother does not let her children stay outside after dark. The fact is that residents do not take much pride in the area. When people do well, they move to better areas. Although the government is trying to improve life for the residents, most people just want to leave.

 ## Text-Dependent Questions

1. What is one of the consequences of vitamin A deficiency?
2. According to the World Health Organization, how many children under the age of five died in 2013? How many of these deaths were due to conditions that could have been prevented?

 ## Research Project

Using your school library or the Internet, do some research to answer the question, "Should governments give more to help poor people?" Some will argue that governments should give poor people more help and greater benefits, to enable them to overcome poverty. Others will say that government should not interfere with people's lives, and that people do better if they are left to themselves. Write a two-page paper with your answer, using examples from your research to support your conclusion, and present it to your class.

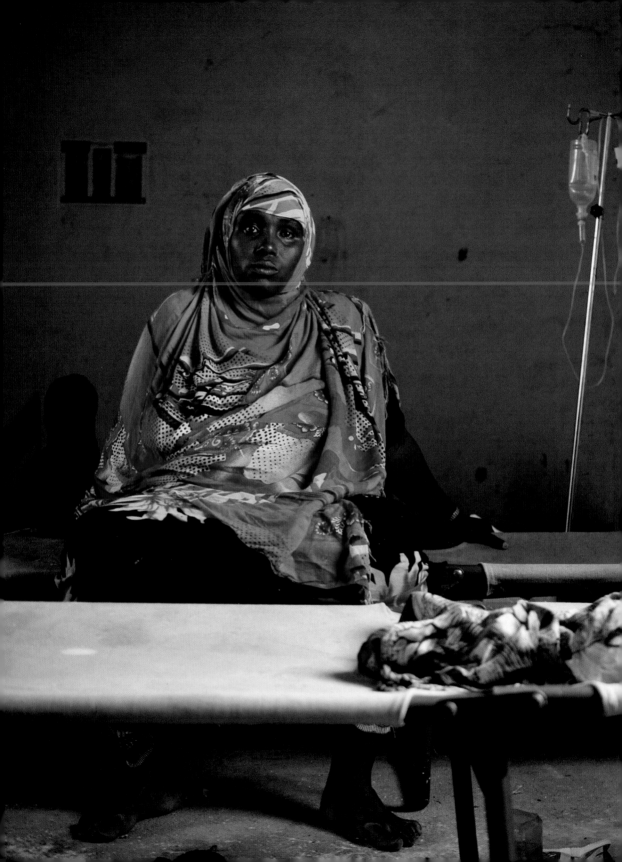

Does Poverty Affect Health?

What is the biggest single health problem in the world today? The World Health Organization has found a surprising answer to this question. The world's biggest killer, and the greatest cause of poor health and suffering, was not cancer, heart disease, or HIV/AIDS. It was extreme poverty.

Based on decades of research, the WHO has found that as the gap between rich and poor widens, so does the difference between rich and poor people's health. The poorest people live shorter, less healthy lives. Even in the wealthiest countries, where people are more likely to have access to hospitals and medicines, those people who live in the poorest areas are more likely to fall ill.

A Somali woman is treated for cholera in a clinic in Belet Weyne, Somalia.

How Does Poverty Affect Life Expectancy?

The WHO found that the links between poverty and bad health were greatest in the *developing world*, especially in the poorest countries or in places affected by wars and conflicts. In such places, even having a baby presents a major health risk. Each year, around half a million women die in pregnancy and childbirth. Nearly all of them come from the poorest countries.

Every year, millions of people die from poverty-related diseases, such as HIV/AIDS, which between 1981 and 2015 had killed nearly 40 million people. Other diseases, such as cholera, Hepatitis B, *malaria*, and typhoid fever, result from unsanitary conditions, which are common where poor people live. Many other diseases that afflict the developing world, such as tuberculosis, polio, diphtheria, tetanus, pertussis, and measles, could be prevented with vaccines that are relatively inexpensive, but often beyond the means of poor families.

 Words to Understand in This Chapter

community—the town, village, suburb or neighborhood we live in, or a feeling of belonging.

developing world—poor countries that are developing their economies and conditions. Richer countries are sometimes called the 'developed world'.

life expectancy—how long a person can expect to live.

malaria—a tropical disease spread by mosquito bites.

shantytown—a town of roughly built dwelling, lacking proper amenities and often built on the edge of a city.

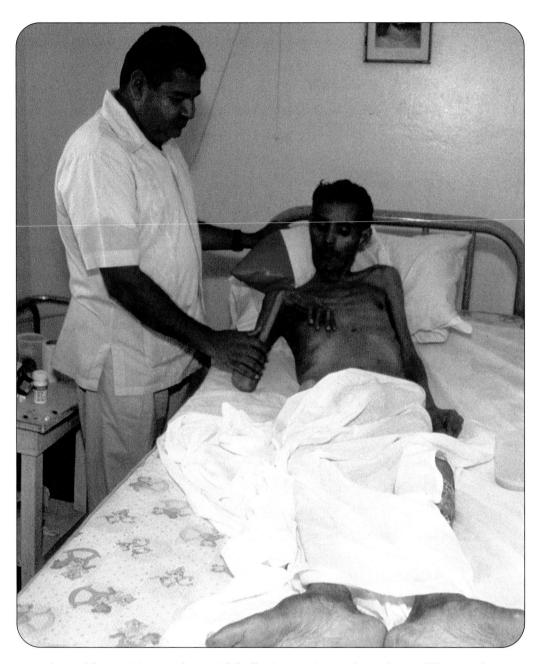

A patient with AIDS in Honduras. Globally, in 2015 an estimated 37 million people were living with HIV or AIDS. Of this number, about 17.4 million are women and 2.6 million are children under age 15, according to data from the World Health Organization.

According to the World Health Organization, a baby born today in a high-income country like the United States or Canada can expect to live 79 years or more. Contrast this with the poorest countries, where the average *life expectancy* is just 62 years. In many African countries, such as Sierra Leone (age 46), Angola (age 51), and Nigeria (age 54), the average life expectancy is much lower.

All the safety nets have collapsed for this homeless man begging on a street in Montreal.

Does Bad Health Cause Poverty?

Poor people are more likely to suffer illness and injury than middle class or wealthy people. But does poverty cause bad health, or does bad health lead to poverty? The answer is complex. Not everyone with a health problem lives in poverty, especially where they have good safety nets such as a supportive family, a regular income, and low-cost, high-quality healthcare. But numerous studies have shown that bad health can be a major factor in pushing people into poverty. This is especially true when society's safety nets are weak or do not exist at all.

Nick lives in the American midwest, one of the wealthiest parts of the world. At the age of 56, he works as a security guard in a local shopping center. It is not a great job, but it is a job and he is glad to have it. However, he is desperately worried about his deteriorating health.

When he was younger Nick had a great life. He had a job, a home, family and friends. He earned good wages by working on the assembly line of a large automobile company. He married Tania and they had two children. They were both working and could take two paid vacations each year.

Then Nick's company closed the factory and moved its operations to another state, where wages were lower. He found a new job, but the wages and working conditions were not as good.

One day he was badly injured. Nick's old job had paid generous benefits to sick workers, but the new company provided few benefits. The family had to depend on Tania's much smaller wage. Before Nick could return to work, his company went

Over the past three decades, companies in the United States, Europe, and other developed nations have closed their manufacturing facilities and moved the operations to other countries where labor costs are lower and there are fewer government regulations. This has meant the loss of good-paying jobs, and the displaced workers often struggle to earn as much as they did before the factory closed.

bankrupt and he was laid off.

After becoming unemployed, Nick spent days in front of the television, eating junk food and smoking. He became overweight, and felt isolated and depressed. Then he had his first heart attack. The doctor said he should give up smoking, eat healthy foods, and lose weight. Nick tried, but he found it too hard to change his lifestyle. Later he suffered a second heart attack.

Facing high medical bills on only one income, Tania also felt under stress and became ill. Nick wanted to work but could not find a job suitable for an older man with health problems. Finally, he took the job in the shopping center, but he is very worried about his heart. He wants to be more healthy, but there is little time for exercise when money is tight and he has to work as much as possible just to support his family.

How Can Poor People Stay Healthy?

What does a *community* need to provide to help people stay healthy? You might suggest such things as doctors and nurses, hospitals and clinics, ambulances, and medicines. Of course, these things are important and necessary. However, it may surprise you to learn that the biggest single improvement in health comes from providing people with safe drinking water, good sanitation, and proper garbage collection.

Having clean water for drinking and washing protects people against germs and infections. Although this may seem obvious, scientists only realized the connection between hygiene and good health in the mid-nineteenth century. And even today, many people around the world live without the conditions for proper hygiene. Why is this?

The simple reason is that poor people cannot afford to build or buy decent facilities themselves, and many governments and private companies cannot, or will not, provide these facilities for them. Hundreds of millions of people live in *shantytowns* or slums without running water, and use open drains for washing. They do not want to live like this, but they have no choice. And if they get sick, they have to treat themselves or find money to pay for medicines.

Why Is Water so Important?

Let us return to Namwinga, the nine-year-old girl from Chipata in Zambia whose story was told in the first chapter of this book. For many years, her family got their water from a local well. They had to stand in line for hours, and, what is more, they had to pay for each bucketful of water that they drew. They boiled water for drinking; if they did not sterilize it thoroughly, bacteria in the water could cause diarrhea and infection. During the rainy season, large puddles near their home became breeding grounds for swarms of mosquitoes, which spread diseases like malaria.

Today, the village of Chipata has clean water, which is pumped from an aquifer deep underground and piped to 42 public tap-stands. People still pay,

 Around 748 million people today still do not have access to an improved source of drinking water, and water demand for manufacturing is expected to increase by 400 per cent between 2000 and 2050 globally.

—The United Nations World Water Development Report 2015

Children draw fresh water from a public well in Peshawar, Pakistan. Safe supplies of drinking water have resulted in many fewer children falling ill from diseases caused by dirty water.

A UNICEF volunteer hands out candies to children in the Democratic Republic of Congo, as part of a vaccination program.

but they make one monthly payment and get much more water. The water supply was planned by CARE International, an international aid agency, that worked with the local government. Local people decided on the location of the tap-stands and helped to lay the pipes. The water is cheap to buy and easy to collect. Best of all, it is clean and healthy.

 ## Text-Dependent Questions

1. What is the average life expectancy of people living in the developed world? What is the average life expectancy of people living in the developing world?
2. What is the biggest single way in which health can be improved in poor communities?

 ## Research Project

Using your school library or the Internet, do some research to answer the question, "Should people be given help to stay healthy?" Keep in mind that there are legitimate arguments on both sides of this debate. Some experts say that healthcare is a public responsibility, and that everyone should be prepared to pay something to help the poorest and the sickest people. Others contend that people must be responsible for their own health, and should not expect others to pay for healthcare. Write a two-page paper with your answer, using examples from your research to support your conclusion, and present it to your class.

Can People Escape Poverty?

Poverty has a devastating effect on the lives of individuals, families and communities. Not only are people deprived of the basic things needed for a good life, they are unable to participate in many areas of society.

So, is poverty inevitable? Will some people always be poor, whatever the situation? We know that throughout history most people have been poor, and there has always been a gap between rich and poor. As we have seen, today's world has more poor people than ever before. However, there are big differences between our situation today and the situation in the past.

Is Poverty Inevitable?

In the past, people lived more isolated, less connected lives. But today, we live in a world linked by fast transport, and by electronic communication devices such as mobile phones, satel-

Christmas dinner at the Los Angeles Mission Homeless Shelter. Poor people can be found even in the wealthiest countries in the world.

lites, email, and the Internet. This means that a change in one part of the world economy can affect even the most remote communities on the other side of the globe, whether for good or bad. It also means that news—for example, of a famine—travels quickly around the world.

Today, we have the knowledge and technology to overcome the worst aspects of poverty. As we have seen, the world already produces more than enough food to feed everybody. Even the poorest country has the potential to deliver basic necessities such as clean water, good sanitation, and electrical power. Modern contraception means that no woman need to have unwanted children, and advances in public health and medicine mean that most babies should survive and grow into healthy adults. Technology offers new ways to provide primary education for young people at a reasonable cost. All these things suggest that we should be able to bring about an end to poverty, and yet poverty continues to affect the lives of millions of people around the world.

 Words to Understand in This Chapter

climate change—manmade changes in the Earth's atmosphere, resulting in rising sea levels and changing weather patterns.

foreign aid—aid given by one country (usually rich) to other countries.

laborers—people working for a wage, usually on a daily basis.

multinational corporation—a large company which operates in more than one country.

pesticides—chemicals used to help crops grow bigger or quicker.

People often ignore the reality of poverty in their communities, just as these pedestrians are walking around a beggar on the sidewalk.

Why Does Poverty Continue?

Although we have the means to ensure that everyone can have a good life, poverty is such a huge problem that there are no easy answers. It is not just a matter of giving money, but changing how people live. Some experts say the problem should be tackled from the top, with more action by national governments as well as by international organizations like the United Nations. Others think that a solution has to begin at the bottom, with actions taken by poor communities themselves.

Humanitarian supplies donated by the United States Agency for International Development (USAID), the American government agency that is responsible for administering most foreign aid. The U.S. government donates to many poor countries—but does such help encourage dependency?

The fact is that it takes action by everyone, including us, if we are to ever really make a difference to the problem of poverty.

Should Governments Do More?

We generally expect our governments to do something to help the poorest people. However, there is a lot of debate about exactly what role governments should play. One view is that governments should have only a small role, providing a framework to enable people to live in safety. The opposite view is that governments should provide a "cradle to grave" welfare service for everyone. Today, most governments have a role somewhere between the two, but the level of social services varies greatly between countries.

The leading donors of foreign aid include some of the wealthiest countries in the world: the United States, the United Kingdom of Great Britain, Germany, France, Japan, Canada, the Netherlands, Australia, Sweden, and Norway.

So, what should governments do for the poorest people? Should they help a lot or a little? Some people say that governments should focus on helping the groups who are unable to help themselves—children, the elderly, the sick and the severely disables. But what about other poor people, such as healthy adults? Do they deserve help as well? Some governments believe that such help creates dependency, rather than encouraging people to help themselves out of poverty. But it can be difficult for poor people to get started without some help.

Afghan girls learn how to sew as part of a vocational training sponsored by the United Nations. Training that enables poor people to develop useful skills provides them with an opportunity to escape poverty.

Let us look again at Chloe's family in Newcastle upon Tyne, which was discussed in chapter four. After Chloe's father left, her mother had to bring up three small children alone. Her mother would have liked to go out to work, but it was just not possible while the children were young. She had to rely instead on benefit payments from the government. When she did look for a job, the wages were so low that she was better off staying on government benefits. But at least she had this safety net, and the security of such things as free healthcare.

To get a better job, Chloe's mother needs more qualifications. Ideally, she would like to be a teacher, but that would involve years of study. Instead, she has taken a job in a call center on the city outskirts. She has to travel some distance but the work is flexible and the government still gives her some benefits that help her make ends meet.

Chloe's mum is smart and resourceful, like most poor people anywhere in the world. But she is fortunate to live in a wealthy country that has a social security system and a strong economy. The poorest countries cannot afford to pay people social security benefits. Many of these countries depend on financial assistance from foreign governments and international organizations just to fund their annual budgets and provide the most basic services.

Some wealthy countries give quite a lot of *foreign aid* and others give much less. But not all the aid goes to the poorest countries. Also, when a foreign government gives aid it often decides how it should be spent. The money might be spent on health and education. But sometimes it ends up being spent on luxury imports for those who can afford them, or supporting *multinational corporations*.

Should poor people help themselves?

If governments cannot solve poverty from the top down, how might poor communities tackle it from the bottom up? Organizations working with poor communities often start by asking people what the biggest problems are in their lives and how they think they can be solved. Sometimes, this approach can help people to take huge steps forward.

Annual floods that occur during the monsoon season in Asia often submerge homes, streets, and farm fields. This flooded city is located in Thailand. Many scientists are concerned that climate change will make flooding more severe, imposing additional hardships on the poor people of this region.

But there are limits to the bottom-up approach. Poverty is such an enormous problem that it demands changes in the way the world is organized.

Let us return to Abu Hameed's village in Bangladesh, mentioned in chapter one. While Abu Hameed comes from one of the richest families, his nine-year-old classmate Kamala comes from one of the poorest. Her family lives in a crowded house that is at risk of being swept away in the annual floods. They own just one bigha of land, and must work as paid *laborers* to survive.

Even so, Kamala's family is better off now than a few years ago. Although they work as laborers, they also have new sources of income. In the past they used their tiny plot of land to grow rice. Today, they also grow vegetables and herbs, and use fewer harmful and expensive *pesticides*. They also grow vegetables on the dikes—the narrow, earth pathways that crisscross flooded rice fields—and use the ponds to breed small fish that eat, and also sell to other farmers.

The poor—both those living in poverty and those just barely above the poverty line—are already the most at risk from climate change. They have the fewest resources to adapt or recovery quickly from shocks.... The damage extreme weather can to do their homes and businesses can prevent the poor from escaping poverty, and it is often the trigger that tips the vulnerable into poverty.

—report by the World Bank, 2016

While Kamala's family has supplied the labor to help themselves, they have been helped by knowledge from outside their community. Special classes supported by CARE International teach poor farmers new methods of farming, and how to work together more effectively. One benefit is an improved diet—the fish and vegetables that Kamala now eats mean that she is no longer malnourished. Her family's higher income also means that Kamala can attend primary school.

Kamala's family now has a more secure life. But they are still very poor. Their livelihood is at risk every time the rivers flood during the monsoon season. The very existence of Bangladesh is threatened because *climate changes* are causing sea levels to rise, which creates flooding. Some of this climate change is caused by pollution from richer countries. Kamala and her family will continue to be under threat unless we make big changes to our world.

Text-Dependent Questions

1. What are two views of governments' role in ending poverty?
2. What factor threatens the existence of low-lying countries like Bangladesh?

 Research Project

Using your school library or the Internet, do some research to answer the question, "Should rich countries provide more financial aid?" Some writers will note that rich countries should be more concerned about poverty outside their borders, and should provide more foreign aid. Others believe that wealthy countries already interfere too much in the affairs of the developing world, and that instead of giving more aid they should eliminate trade barriers and buy more goods from poor countries. Write a two-page paper with your answer, using examples from your research to support your conclusion, and present it to your class.

7

Can We End Poverty Worldwide?

Poverty affects the lives of billions of people worldwide. It involves complex issues such as employment, trade, foreign financial aid, and debt. It requires big solutions, involving everyone from the United Nations and the world's governments, companies, banks, and charities, right down to communities and individuals.

We have already talked about the role of governments and some of the steps they can take to end poverty in their own countries. But responsibilities do not end there. Every government needs to look beyond their borders to the wider world.

Each year, millions of people *emigrate* to work in wealthy countries, often illegally and at great danger to themselves. Most send money home to their families. These funds, known as *remittances*, often become a vital part of their home coun-

Donating food or non-perishable items to a local food bank, or volunteering your time to work in one of these facilities, is a small step you can take to combat poverty in your community.

try's economy. Millions more people would migrate if they were allowed to. Helping poor countries to build more prosperous economies would not stop migration, but it would provide more opportunities for people to stay in their own countries.

How Can Banks Help?

Private companies often regard poverty as being outside their responsibilities. But today the biggest multinational companies operate on a worldwide basis. They may have their headquarters in one country and their factories, offices, shops and customers in dozens of others. By shifting production from one city or one country to another, companies are responsible for creating or destroying thousands of jobs. Their decisions affect the lives of people too poor to buy their products.

Banks rarely develop services for poor communities. Billions of people go through life without accumulating savings or opening a bank account. It is poor people who find it hardest to borrow money and who must pay the highest rates of interest. Yet experience has shown that small loans at low

 Words to Understand in This Chapter

emigrate—to leave a native country in order to live and work in another country.

non-governmental organization (NGO)—a citizen-based group that works to improve society, rather than make a profit.

remittance—the practice of sending money home to family in another country to help support them.

Men line up to vote in a presidential election in Afghanistan. The increase in the number of democratic elections taking place in Asia and Africa encourages many Western leaders, who believe good governance is essential to ending poverty in these regions.

interest rates have enabled some of the poorest people to harness their own skills and enterprise, and use them to rise from poverty.

Often, new ideas to tackle poverty come from charities and organizations that work with poor communities. They learn from experience what works and what does not. The lesson for governments, banks, and companies is a simple one: listen to the people who really matter—the poor.

Can One Person Make a Difference?

Is there anything that you, as an individual, can do about poverty? After all, poverty is such a big, complex problem it may seem best just to leave it to others. One person, working alone, may not feel they can make much impact. But together there is a lot that ordinary people can accomplish.

The first step is to be aware of poverty, whether it is in our own community or overseas, and to make others aware of it. Democratic governments do respond to public opinion. If people express their thoughts and feelings loudly and strongly enough, for long enough, governments will start to take action.

Public pressure to do more to help developing countries has grown in recent years as individuals and organizations formed in wealthy countries have held rallies and events urging public leaders to take action. One well-known activist is the rock star Bono, of the band U2. During the 2000s Bono formed a group called DATA (which stands for Debt, AIDS, Trade, Africa) that advocated for debt forgiveness for poor African countries. The Drop the Debt campaign was an organization with similar goals.

Both Drop the Debt and DATA eventually became part of the ONE campaign, an international organization that currently fights extreme poverty and preventable disease. In addition to debt relief, the ONE campaign has programs that support many initiatives related to eradicating poverty. These include development projects to bring clean water to rural villages and provide schools and teachers for poor communities. The organ-

Loans for a Better Life

In 1976, the Grameen Bank of Bangladesh started to make small loans to poor rural women without land or property. The women used the loans to buy goats or chickens, or to set up as small traders. They used the income they made for food, healthcare, and their children's education. Interest rates were low and loans were repaid on time. Today, the Grameen Bank has more than 2,500 branches, and similar schemes are run in over 40 different countries. The bank and its founder, Muhammad Yunus, received the Nobel Peace Prize in 2006 for its contributions to eradicating poverty.

United Nations Secretary-General Ban Ki-moon meets with Grameen Bank founder Muhammed Yunus (right).

Ten Live 8 concerts were held in July 2005 just before the G8 summit, a meeting of eight countries with large economies. Organizers of the events hoped to educate the public about poverty in Africa and pressure leaders of wealthy nations to agree to debt cancellation, establishment of fair world trade practices, and giving of additional foreign aid. This concert is in London's Hyde Park.

ization funds medical clinics and vaccinates people against preventable diseases. It also works to reduce government corruption that prevents foreign aid from helping the poorest people, and supports measures that enable farmers to earn a fairer price for their crops.

However, the ONE campaign and other *non-governmental organizations (NGOs)* have noted that much more remains to be done. Despite debt relief, many poor countries still owe substantial money to wealthy nations, paying an estimated $100 million each day in debt repayments. There is still a long way to go, but today the issue is on the world agenda and will not go away.

How Can I Help?

There are many other things we can do as individuals. We can campaign for our governments to take action to enable people to escape poverty. We can call on them to offer the poorest people support in obtaining work, education, and a better, safer environment.

Rock star and social activist Bono speaks at an international conference on ending poverty.

We can support charities who give practical help, and movements who campaign for changes in laws and attitudes. We can ask banks and businesses to include poor communities in their plans, rather than exclude them. We can buy goods—such as coffee, tea and cocoa—where the labels tell us that the producers are paid a fair price. We can support enterprises run by poor communities, where workers are paid a living wage. We can raise funds in our schools and communities for good causes and campaigns against poverty.

There is a lot we can do to fight poverty, and there has never been a better time to start.

Text-Dependent Questions

1. What funds, sent by workers home to their families, become a vital part of their home country's economy?
2. What is the first step for an individual to work toward solving the problem of poverty?
3. How much do poor countries pay each day in debt repayments?

 Research Project

In 2000, the United Nations created the Millennium Development Goals (MDGs), a set of eight goals ranging from cutting the rate of absolute poverty in half to providing universal primary education. The target date for accomplishing these goals was 2015. Using the Internet and your school library, do some research on the MDGs. Which of the goals were accomplished by the deadline, and which were not? Why? Write a short report about the success or failure of this program, and include information about next steps that the United Nations and other international organizations might take in these areas.

U.S. Census Bureau Data on Poverty in the United States

In 2014, the official poverty rate in the United States was 14.8 percent, according to data collected by the U.S. Census Bureau and reported in early 2016. The Bureau found that at the end of 2014 there were 46.7 million Americans living in poverty. Neither the poverty rate nor the number of people in poverty had changed much from from the Census Bureau's 2013 estimates. In fact, the Census Bureau found, the poverty rate in the United States has been essentially unchanged since about 2011.

The 2014 poverty rate was 2.3 percentage points higher than the poverty rate in 2007. During that year, a crisis in the mortgage banking industry led to an economic recession from which the United States, as well as the global economy, has not yet fully recovered.

A homeless man sleeps on the sidewalk in the affluent neighborhood of Beverly Hills, California. Data on poverty in the United States reported in this appendix is adapted from a U.S. Census Bureau report issued in September 2015 titled Income and Poverty in the United States: 2014, *by Carmen DeNavas-Walt and Bernadette D. Proctor.*

Poverty by Racial or Ethnic Group

The poverty rate for non-Hispanic Whites was 10.1 percent in 2014. That is lower than the poverty rates for other racial or ethnic groups. Non-Hispanic Whites accounted for 61.8 percent of the total U.S. population, and made up 42.1 percent of the people in poverty. For non-Hispanic Whites, neither the poverty rate nor the number of people in poverty experienced a statistically significant change between 2013 and 2014.

African Americans had the highest poverty rate in 2014, at 26.2 percent. The Census Bureau found that there were 10.8 million African Americans living in poverty. For Asians, the 2014 poverty rate was 12 percent, which represented 2.1 million people in poverty. Among Hispanics, the 2014 poverty rate was 23.6 percent and there were 13.1 million people in poverty. None of these estimates were statistically different from the 2013 estimates.

Poverty by Age Category and Gender

In 2014, 13.5 percent of people aged 18 to 64 (a total of 26.5 million people) were living in poverty, compared with 10 percent of people aged 65 and older (4.6 million). That year, 21.1 percent of children under age 18 (15.5 million children) were living in poverty. Children represented 23.3 percent of the total U.S. population in 2014, and made up 33.3 percent of the total number of Americans living in poverty.

The Census Bureau defines "related children" as people under age 18 who are related to the householder by birth, marriage, or adoption who are not themselves householders or

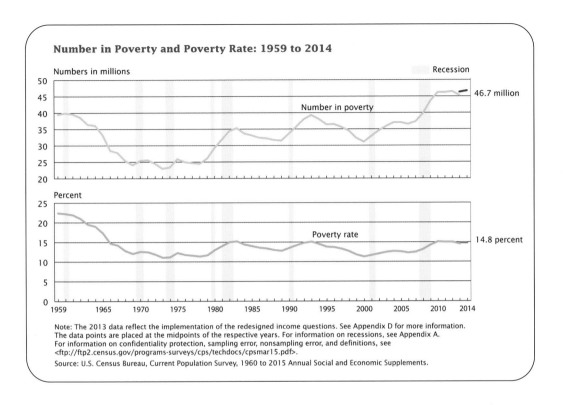

Number in Poverty and Poverty Rate: 1959 to 2014

Numbers in millions

Recession

Number in poverty

46.7 million

Percent

Poverty rate

14.8 percent

1959 1965 1970 1975 1980 1985 1990 1995 2000 2005 2010 2014

Note: The 2013 data reflect the implementation of the redesigned income questions. See Appendix D for more information. The data points are placed at the midpoints of the respective years. For information on recessions, see Appendix A. For information on confidentiality protection, sampling error, nonsampling error, and definitions, see <ftp://ftp2.census.gov/programs-surveys/cps/techdocs/cpsmar15.pdf>.

Source: U.S. Census Bureau, Current Population Survey, 1960 to 2015 Annual Social and Economic Supplements.

spouses of householders. The poverty rate for all related children under age 18 was 20.7 percent, for a total of 15 million children living in poverty with their families in 2014. The problem is worse in single-parent households, particularly if that parent is the mother. For related children in families with a female householder, 46.5 percent were in poverty, compared with 10.6 percent of related children in married-couple families.

The poverty rate and the number in poverty for related children under age 6 were 23.5 percent and 5.5 million in 2014. More than half (55.1 percent) of related children under age 6 in families with a female householder were in poverty. This was more than four times the rate of their counterparts in mar-

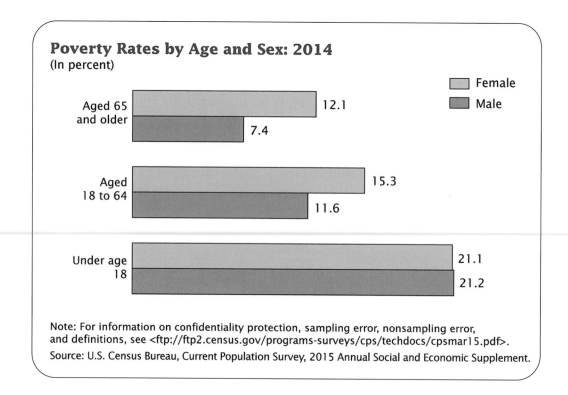

Poverty Rates by Age and Sex: 2014
(In percent)

Female
Male

Aged 65 and older
12.1
7.4

Aged 18 to 64
15.3
11.6

Under age 18
21.1
21.2

Note: For information on confidentiality protection, sampling error, nonsampling error, and definitions, see <ftp://ftp2.census.gov/programs-surveys/cps/techdocs/cpsmar15.pdf>.
Source: U.S. Census Bureau, Current Population Survey, 2015 Annual Social and Economic Supplement.

ried-couple families (11.6 percent).

In 2014, 13.4 percent of males and 16.1 percent of females were in poverty. Neither poverty rate showed a statistically significant change from the Census Bureau's 2013 estimate.

Gender differences in poverty rates were more pronounced for those aged 65 and older. The poverty rate for women aged 65 and older was 12.1 percent, while the poverty rate for men aged 65 and older was 7.4 percent. The poverty rate for women aged 18 to 64 was 15.3 percent while the poverty rate for men aged 18 to 64 was 11.6 percent. For children under age 18, the poverty rate for girls (21.1 percent) was not statistically different from the poverty rate for boys (21.2 percent).

Poverty by Region and Residence

None of the four regions of the United States (Northeast, South, Midwest, and West) experienced a significant change in the poverty rate or the number of people in poverty between 2013 and 2014. In 2014, the poverty rate was 12.6 percent for the Northeast, representing 7 million people in poverty; 13 percent for the Midwest (8.7 million in poverty); 16.5 percent for the South (19.5 million in poverty); and 15.2 percent for the West (11.4 million in poverty). The South has traditionally had a higher poverty rate than the other three regions.

Inside metropolitan statistical areas, the poverty rate was 14.5 percent, representing 38.4 million people living in poverty in 2014. The rate for those who live in the suburbs—within the metropolitan area, but not in the principal city—was lower than the overall rate for the metropolitan area at 11.8 percent (representing 19.7 million people). Correspondingly, the poverty rate for those who lived in principal cities was 18.9 percent, representing 18.7 million people.

Among those living in rural areas, the poverty rate was 16.5 percent, with 8.2 million living in poverty in 2014.

International Organizations

United Nations High Commissioner for Human Rights
Administrative Section
Office of the United Nations
High Commissioner for Human Rights
Palais des Nations
CH-1211 Geneva 10, Switzerland
Phone: + 41 22 917 90 20
E-mail: InfoDesk@ohchr.org
Website: http://www.ohchr.org/english

Amnesty International
5 Penn Plaza
14th Floor
New York, NY 10001
Phone: (212) 807-8400
E-mail: aimember@aiusa.org
Website: http://www.amnestyusa.org

Human Rights Watch
350 Fifth Ave.
34th Floor
New York, NY 10118-3299
Phone: (212) 290-4700
E-mail: hrwnyc@hrw.org
Website: http://www.hrw.org

The Abolish Slavery Coalition

8620 W Third St.

Los Angeles, CA 90048

E-mail: richard@abolishslavery.org

Website: http://www.abolishslavery.org

African Commission on Human and Peoples' Rights

31 Bijilo Annex Layout, Kombo North District

Western Region P.O. Box 673 Banjul

The Gambia

Phone: (220) 441 05 05

E-mail: au-banjul@africa-union.org

Website: http://www.achpr.org

Series Glossary

apartheid—literally meaning "apartness," the political policies of the South African government from 1948 until the early 1990s designed to keep peoples segregated based on their color.

BCE and CE—alternatives to the traditional Western designation of calendar eras, which used the birth of Jesus as a dividing line. BCE stands for "Before the Common Era," and is equivalent to BC ("Before Christ"). Dates labeled CE, or "Common Era," are equivalent to *Anno Domini* (AD, or "the Year of Our Lord").

colony—a country or region ruled by another country.

democracy—a country in which the people can vote to choose those who govern them.

detention center—a place where people claiming asylum and refugee status are held while their case is investigated.

ethnic cleansing—an attempt to rid a country or region of a particular ethnic group. The term was first used to describe the attempt by Serb nationalists to rid Bosnia of Muslims.

house arrest—to be detained in your own home, rather than in prison, under the constant watch of police or other government forces, such as the army.

reformist—a person who wants to improve a country or an institution, such as the police force, by ridding it of abuses or faults.

republic—a country without a king or queen, such as the US.

United Nations—an international organization set up after the end of World War II to promote peace and co-operation throughout the world. Its predecessor was the League of Nations.

UN Security Council—the permanent committee of the United Nations that oversees its peacekeeping operations around the world.

World Bank—an international financial organization, connected to the United Nations. It is the largest source of financial aid to developing countries.

World War I—A war fought in Europe from 1914 to 1918, in which an alliance of nations that included Great Britain, France, Russia, Italy, and the United States defeated the alliance of Germany, Austria-Hungary, the Ottoman Empire, and Bulgaria.

World War II—A war fought in Europe, Africa, and Asia from 1939 to 1945, in which the Allied Powers (the United States, Great Britain, France, the Soviet Union, and China) worked together to defeat the Axis Powers (Germany, Italy, and Japan).

Further Reading

Acemoglu, Daron, and James A. Robinson. *Why Nations Fail: The Origins of Power, Prosperity, and Poverty*. New York: Crown Business, 2012.

Banerjee, Abhijit, and Esther Duflo. *Poor Economics: A Radical Rethinking of the Way to Fight Global Poverty*. New York: Public Affairs, 2011.

Beeson, Mark, and Nick Bisley. *Issues in 21st Century World Politics*. New York: Palgrave Macmilan, 2013.

Fedorak, Shirley A. *Global Issues: A Cross-Cultural Perspective*. Toronto: University of Toronto Press, 2012.

Hulme, David. *Global Poverty: Global Governance and Poor People in the Post-2015 Era*. New York: Routledge, 2015.

McMahon, Paul. *Feeding Frenzy: Land Grabs, Price Spikes, and the World Food Crisis*. London: Profile Books, 2014.

Internet Resources

http://www.one.org/us

The ONE campaign is an international advocacy organization that works to end extreme poverty and preventable disease throughout the world.

http://www.care.org

CARE is a humanitarian organization that provides disaster relief and fights poverty around the world.

https://www.usaid.gov

USAID is the lead U.S. Government agency that works to end extreme global poverty. It implements U.S. foreign aid to expand stable and free societies, create markets and trade partners for the United States, and foster good will abroad.

https://www.cia.gov/library/publications/the-world-factbook

The CIA World Factbook website provides a great deal of statistical information about all of the world's countries. It is regularly updated.

www.un.org/english

The English-language web page for the United Nations can be searched for stories and information related to all of the world's countries, as well as on U.N. programs and initiatives.

www.bbc.com/news

The official website of BBC News provides articles and videos on important international news and world events.

http://www.who.int/en/

The World Health Organization monitors international health systems and provides leadership on matters critical to health care throughout the world.

http://www.census.gov/hhes/www/poverty/data/incpovhlth/2014/index.html

The U.S. Census Bureau provides links to its annual reports on poverty and household income in the United States at this Web page.

Index

Numbers in **bold italics** refer to captions.

About the Author

Karen Steinman works with CARE International, one of the world's leading relief and development agencies. She has written more than 10 books for young people on social issues.

Eager Street Academy #884
401 East Eager Street
Baltimore, MD 21202